Bugs in our Homes

Written by Jill Eggleton

T0351221

Contents

Bugs in our homes

Millions of bugs live in our homes. Some come and decide to stay for good. Others just stay for a short while. Some spend their whole lives in houses. Others come and go, depending on the season. They are all uninvited **guests**!

For a bug, each room has a different **environment**. The kitchen offers warmth. The bathroom can be as **humid** as a rainforest. Bedrooms have dark, cave-like cupboards and drawers. The living room can be like a desert – vast and dry.

House-loving bugs choose the environment and food supplies that suit them best.

Close-up of a woodlouse

Kitchen bugs

Some bugs feel at home in the kitchen because it has a range of **climates**. It's warm behind the oven and refrigerator, damp around the sink, and dry and dark in the cupboards.

Bugs get into a kitchen through windows and doors, up drainpipes, through gaps in the floor and walls, and with food. If air can get in, so can bugs!

A wasp eating jam

Bugs eat food that is left lying around in a kitchen. They can survive by eating just the tiniest crumb of food, and drinking the smallest drop of water.

Cockroaches

Cockroaches like to live in cracks and **crevices** in kitchens. They come out at night. When daylight comes, they scurry back into the dark, moist and warm places behind ovens and fridges. Here, they usually huddle together in groups.

Cockroaches often feed in groups, too, although they do not share food with each other. They eat anything – meat, milk and cheese, sweets, glue, books, and even tomato ketchup!

If cockroaches feel threatened when feeding, the hairs on the small 'bumps' near their tails give them the message to run.

Yum - tomato ketchup!

Weevils

Weevils can be found in dry foods like flour and rice. They can get into the kitchen in packets bought from shops. If a weevil is caught, it will pretend to be dead for a while, and then slowly walk away!

A weevil

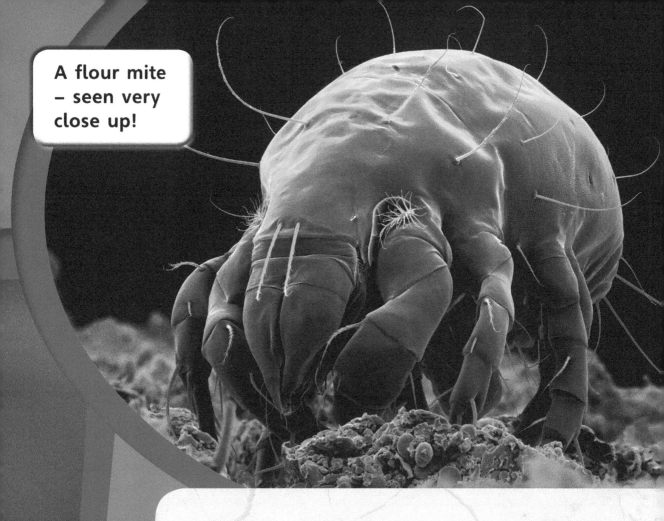

A flour mite – seen very close up!

Mites

Mites are often found in cornflakes, flour, cheese and dried fruit. They look like specks of dust. If mites are seen in food it means that the food is being kept in a damp place.

People can check for mites in food such as flour by spreading the flour onto a sheet of paper. If there are mites, the flour will become lumpy as the mites start to move.

Living-room bugs

Living-room bugs like a dry environment. There could be bugs eating your books, or nibbling wallpaper or the carpet. There could be bugs in your television, curtains or chairs. Most come out at night.

Silverfish

Silverfish have been around for a very long time. They were probably already on Earth when the first fish left the water and joined the dinosaurs on land.

Although silverfish prefer humid places, they can be found in living rooms because they like to eat books, paper, glue, carpet and fabrics on furniture. They could eat a whole stamp collection!

Book lice

Book lice don't eat books like silverfish do, but they do feed on glue and the invisible **mould** that grows on the paper in books that are damp.

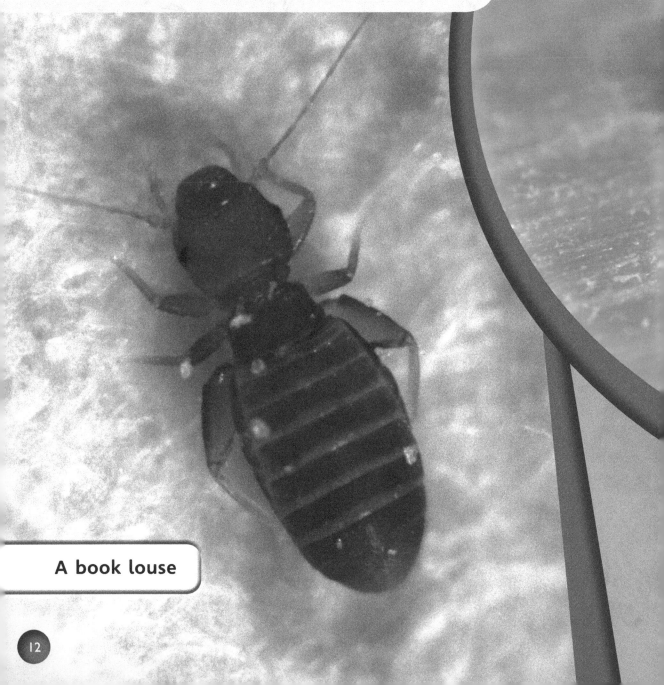

A book louse

Carpet beetles

Carpet beetles are very hard to find. They burrow deep into the carpet to lay their eggs. It is their **larvae** that do the most damage – they can eat holes in the carpet.

Bedroom bugs

Many bugs come uninvited into the bedroom. They make their homes in beds, cupboards and in the clothes in drawers.

Dust mites on a piece of material, seen through a microscope

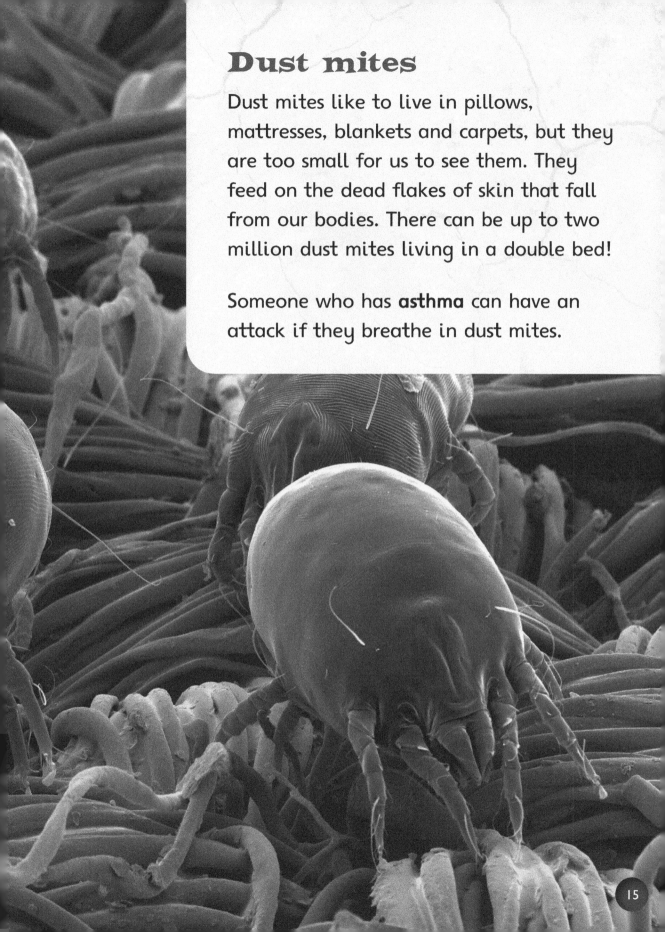

Dust mites

Dust mites like to live in pillows, mattresses, blankets and carpets, but they are too small for us to see them. They feed on the dead flakes of skin that fall from our bodies. There can be up to two million dust mites living in a double bed!

Someone who has **asthma** can have an attack if they breathe in dust mites.

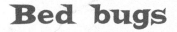
Bed bugs

Bed bugs are blood-sucking bedroom invaders. They can suck up to seven times their own body weight in ten minutes!

They usually hide in a crack in the wall near the bed and don't come out until they're hungry.

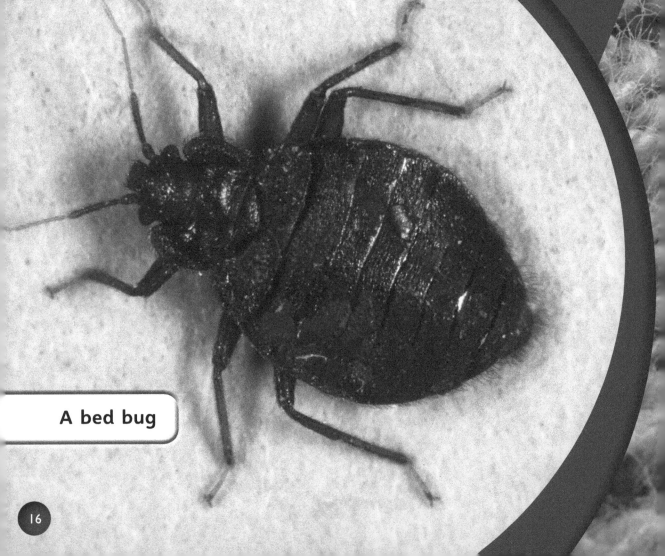

A bed bug

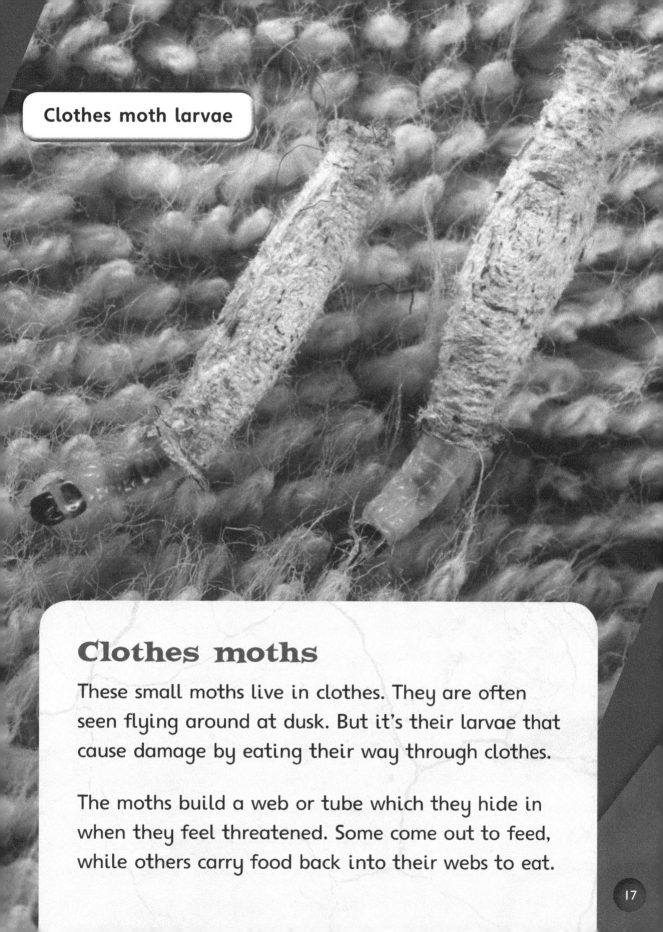

Clothes moth larvae

Clothes moths

These small moths live in clothes. They are often seen flying around at dusk. But it's their larvae that cause damage by eating their way through clothes.

The moths build a web or tube which they hide in when they feel threatened. Some come out to feed, while others carry food back into their webs to eat.

Bathroom bugs

Bathroom bugs like a damp, humid home. For a bug, a bathroom can be like a rain forest – always damp. It can be a good home for larvae that need damp conditions to live in.

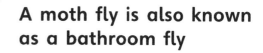

A moth fly is also known as a bathroom fly

Moth flies

Moth flies are very small bugs that can be seen resting on a bathroom wall, or in the sink or bath during the day. They become active at night.

They lay their eggs in the damp, sludgy slime that gathers around the plug hole. The larvae feed on **bacteria** and **fungi.**

These tiny flies are more of a nuisance than a danger. They don't sting, bite, or cause any damage.

19

Bugs that are everywhere!

Fleas

Fleas are a real pest and can be found anywhere in the house. They are **parasites**. They bite and suck up blood and only live on animals that are warm-blooded – including humans.

Cat and dog fleas are smaller than a pinhead. Fleas that live on people are slightly bigger. Fleas can lay around 30 eggs a day – that's a lot of fleas in one house!

A flea sucking blood

Flies

The house fly is a pest that can spread many diseases.

Flies breed in decaying food and manure heaps, and other places where their maggots can find food.

Flies can go straight from a manure heap to a house, where they land on food. This is how they spread disease. Many flies find food in houses by smelling it.

A house spider and fly

Spiders

Spiders can be found in every room in a house. They make webs across windows, in corners and high up on walls.

All spiders are **predators**. Some can even become **cannibals** if their living space becomes crowded. But spiders can be useful as they eat other insects you don't want in your house, such as flies.

Mosquitoes

Mosquitoes can be deadly because they can carry diseases. In some places in the world, many people die every year from **malaria**, which they catch from mosquito bites.

In Britain, most mosquitoes feed on animals, but some bite humans, too. Only the females bite and suck blood because they need blood for their eggs to develop.

Mosquitoes use their **antennae** to track down the warmth, smell and sweat of humans and animals. They suck up blood through their **proboscis**. They need their victims to be still so that the proboscis is not damaged.

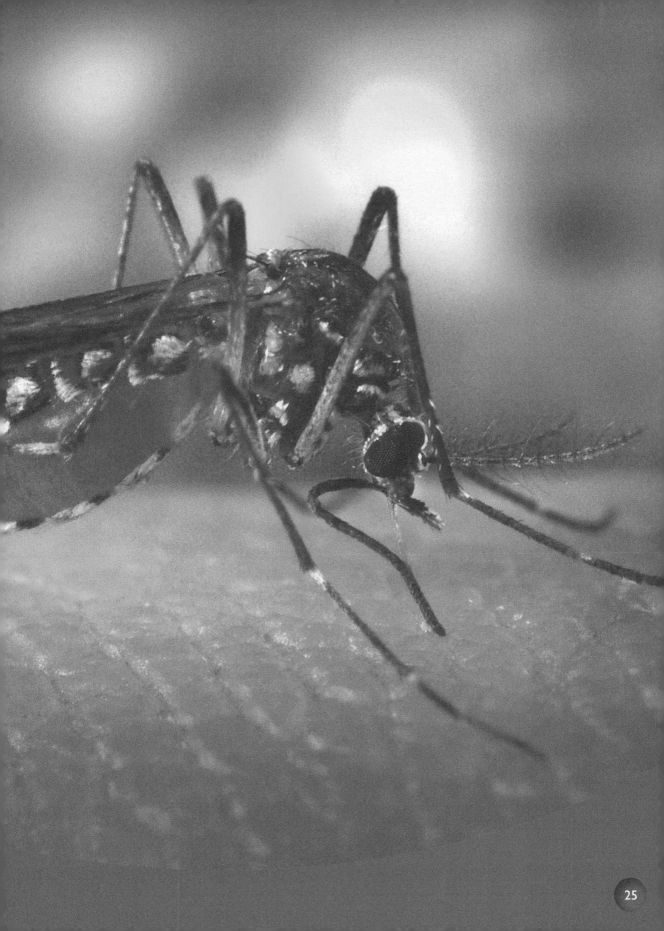

A perfect home!

Bugs choose the homes and food supplies that suit them best.

In their natural environments, bugs such as ants and spiders can be useful. As uninvited guests in our houses, they can be a nuisance. Some bugs even spread diseases.

It is very difficult to make a house 'bug proof'. Creepy, crawly, uninvited guests will always find a way in.

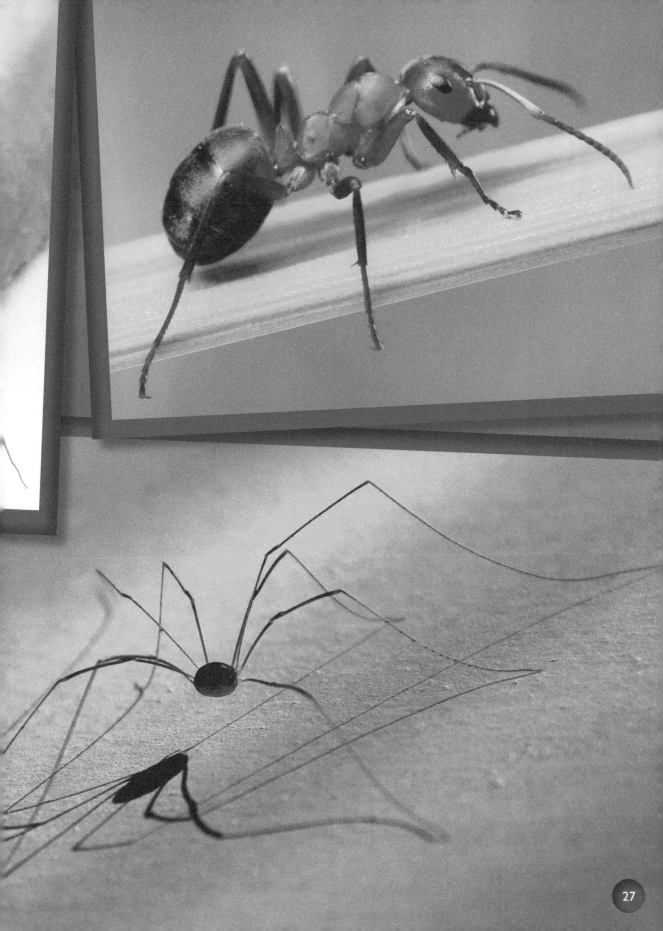

Crazy
cockroach facts

A cockroach can go for a month without food.

A cockroach can live for a week without water.

A cockroach can live for at least a week without its head!

A cockroach can swim, and can hold its breath for 40 minutes.

A cockroach has claws on its feet to help it climb walls.

A cockroach's eyes can see in all directions at the same time.

Fantastic
flea facts

A flea can jump 200 times its own body length.

If a flea were the size of a human, it could jump over a skyscraper.

A flea can somersault over and over in mid-air.

A flea has large eyes, but can only tell if it's light or dark.

'Flea circuses' were popular from the 1830s to the 1930s.

The name of the game 'tiddlywinks' means 'the game of the flea' in fifteen different languages.

Quiz

1 When do cockroaches come out to look for food?

  a Midday

  b Early in the morning

  c At night

2 What does a weevil do if it is caught?

  a It stands on its back legs.

  b It tries to run away.

  c It pretends to be dead.

3 What do book lice like to eat?

  a Apples and bananas

  b Glue and mould

  c Chocolate and sweets

4 How many eggs can a flea lay every day?

  a About 5

  b About 100

  c About 30

Answers on page 31

Glossary

antennae	feelers on heads of insects
asthma	disease that makes it difficult to breathe
bacteria	the most simple living things, which help material to rot and change
cannibals	animals that eat their own species
climates	consist of temperature and humidity
crevices	narrow openings
environment	surroundings
fungi	plants such as toadstools, mushrooms, mould
guests	people (or animals) invited into a person's house
humid	moist, damp
larvae	grubs; the young of insects
malaria	fever from mosquito bite
mould	growth on old food and other material
parasites	insects that live and feed on others
predators	animals that hunt and eat other animals
proboscis	tube on the head that acts like a mouth

Quiz answers: 1c; 2c; 3b; 4c

Index